THIS CANDLEWICK BOOK BELONGS TO:

_____

_____

_____

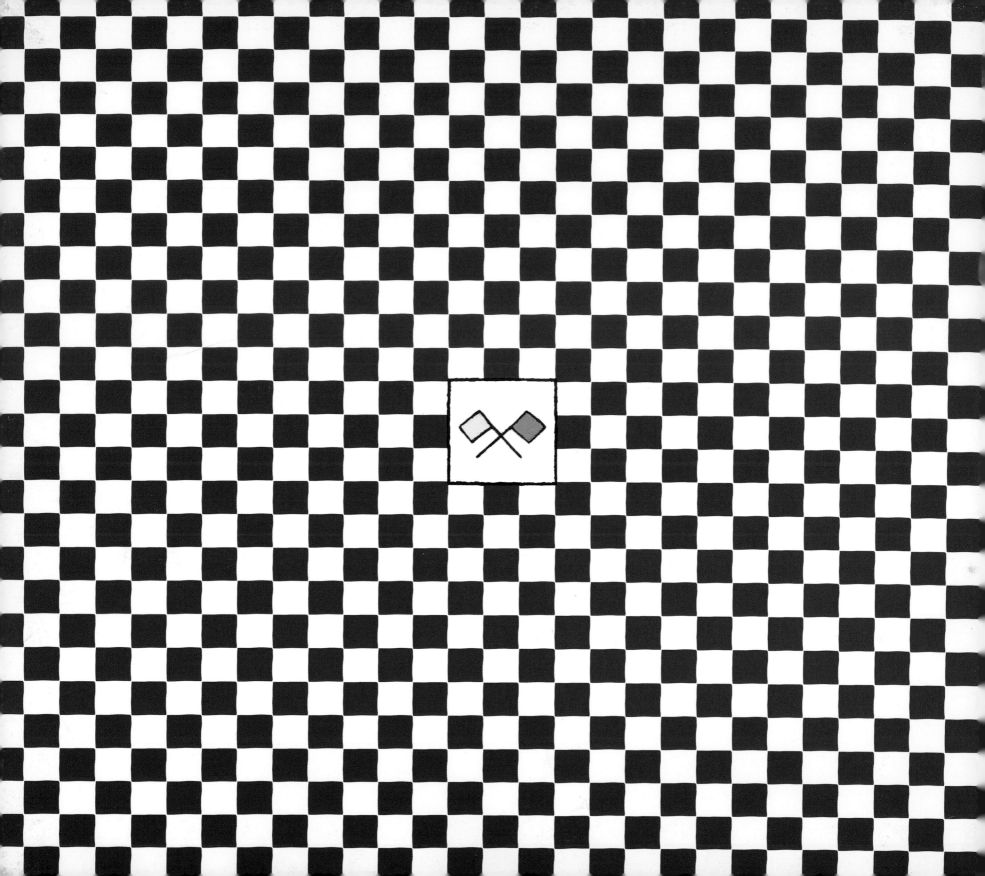

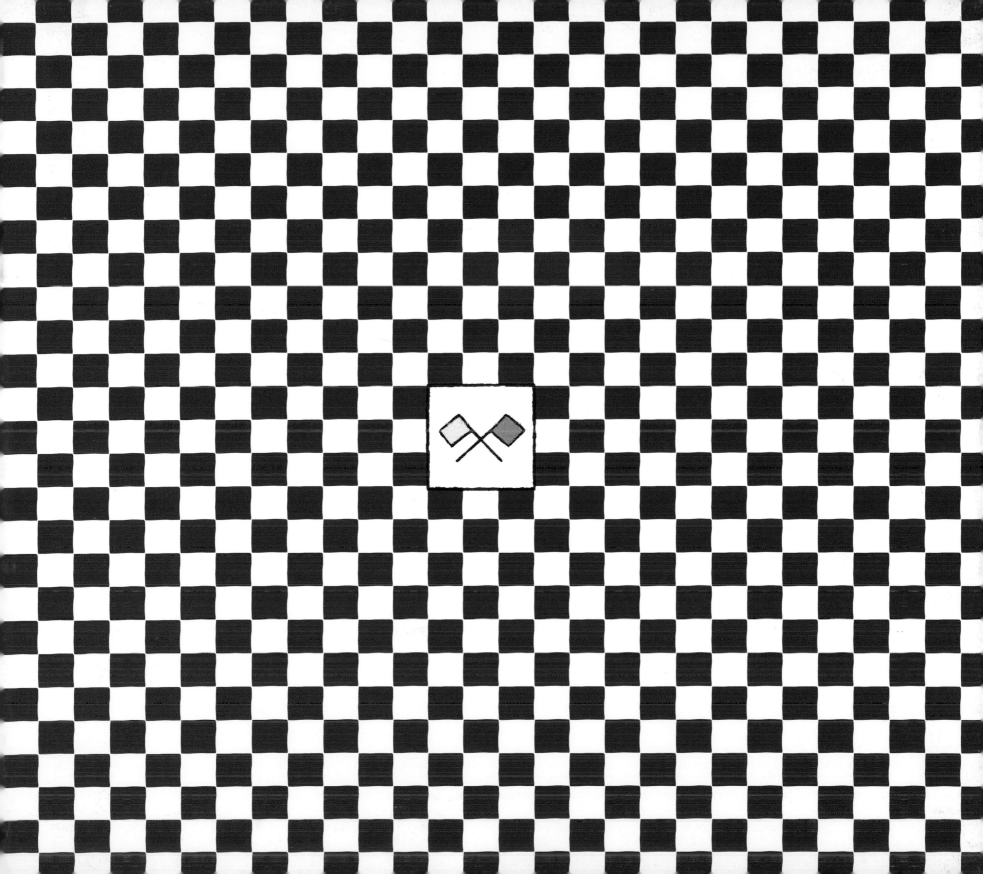

For Great Dividers everywhere
D. D.

To my family
and Dixie and Grover
T. M.

Text copyright © 1999 by Dayle Ann Dodds
Illustrations copyright © 1999 by Tracy Mitchell

First paperback edition 2005

The Library of Congress has cataloged the hardcover edition as follows:
Dodds, Dayle Ann.
The Great Divide / Dayle Ann Dodds ;
illustrated by Tracy Mitchell. —1st ed.
p.   cm.
Summary: Eighty people begin to race in the Great Divide,
but each new challenge divides the number of racers in half.
ISBN 0-7636-0442-9 (hardcover)
[1. Racing—Fiction. 2. Divison—Fiction. 3. Stories in rhyme.]
I. Mitchell, Tracy, ill. II. Title.
PZ8.3.D645Gr   1999
[E]—dc21   98-35833

ISBN 0-7636-1592-7 (paperback)

2 4 6 8 10 9 7 5 3 1

Printed in China

This book was typeset in Handwriter.
The illustrations were done in acrylic on modeling paste.

Candlewick Press
2067 Massachusetts Avenue
Cambridge, Massachusetts 02140

visit us at www.candlewick.com

The Great Divide

Dayle Ann Dodds

illustrated by

Tracy Mitchell

CANDLEWICK PRESS
CAMBRIDGE, MASSACHUSETTS

"BANG!" GOES THE GUN. THE RACE IS ON.

A CLOUD OF DUST.
THEY'RE HERE—
THEY'RE GONE...

Pushing and pedaling side by side,

eighty begin The Great Divide.

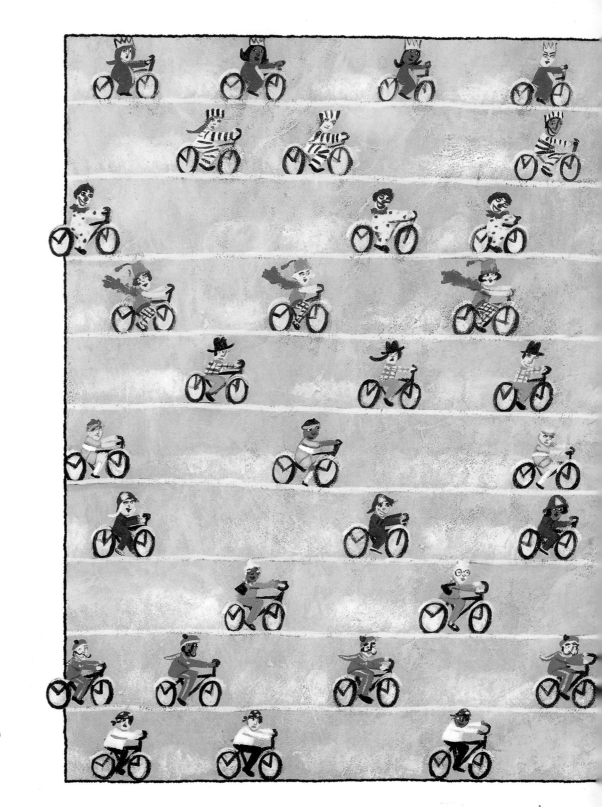

Just up ahead, just beyond sight,
one path leads left,
one path leads right.

Split by a canyon so deep
and so wide, the

riders must

part at

The

Great

D

i

v

i

d

e

Half take a tumble.
Their tires go

pop!

Half carry on,
never to stop.

On with the race.
Head for a boat!

Forty racers
now have to float!

What's up ahead?
A loud, roaring sound!
Whooshing whirlpools
spin all around.

Half are swept up
in a dizzying whirl.
Half battle on through
foam and swirl.

Out of the river,
onto dry land,

twenty racers
take to the sand.

One path turns east.
One path turns west.
Split by a mountain,
which choice is best?

Half stampede west
to a muddy disgrace.
Half gallop east
at a thunderous pace.

In hot air balloons
floating up high,

10

ten racers
now sail through
the sky!

Half blow north
right into a storm.
Half breeze south,
safe and warm.

5

Five press on,
pushing danger aside,
determined to win
The Great Divide.

Into the city,
down the main street,
they're racing on foot—
they're in a dead heat.

One runner stops
with a rock in her shoe.

Four are now left,
split two and two.

Pedaling bicycles—
one to each pair—
they zoom on ahead
as fast as they dare.

So fast, in fact, they
can't find the brake.
With a crash
and a splash
they fall in the lake!

A hush fills the crowd.
They look far.
They look near.
Are there no racers left?
Have they no one to cheer?

LINE!

Are there zero left over?
Are there zilch?
Are there none?
Not one? Not any?
Is the race done?

Wait!

Up in the sky—
what could it be?
Roaring!
Soaring!
Who do they see?

With a wave
of her hand,
with a dip
and a glide,

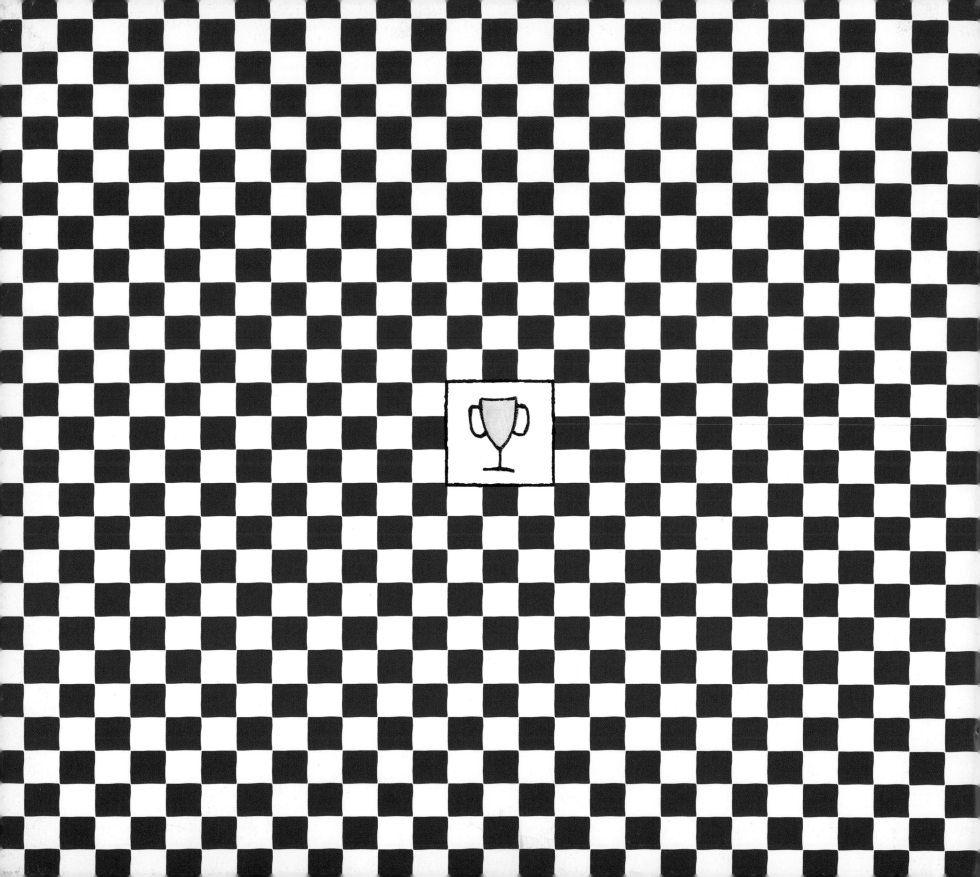

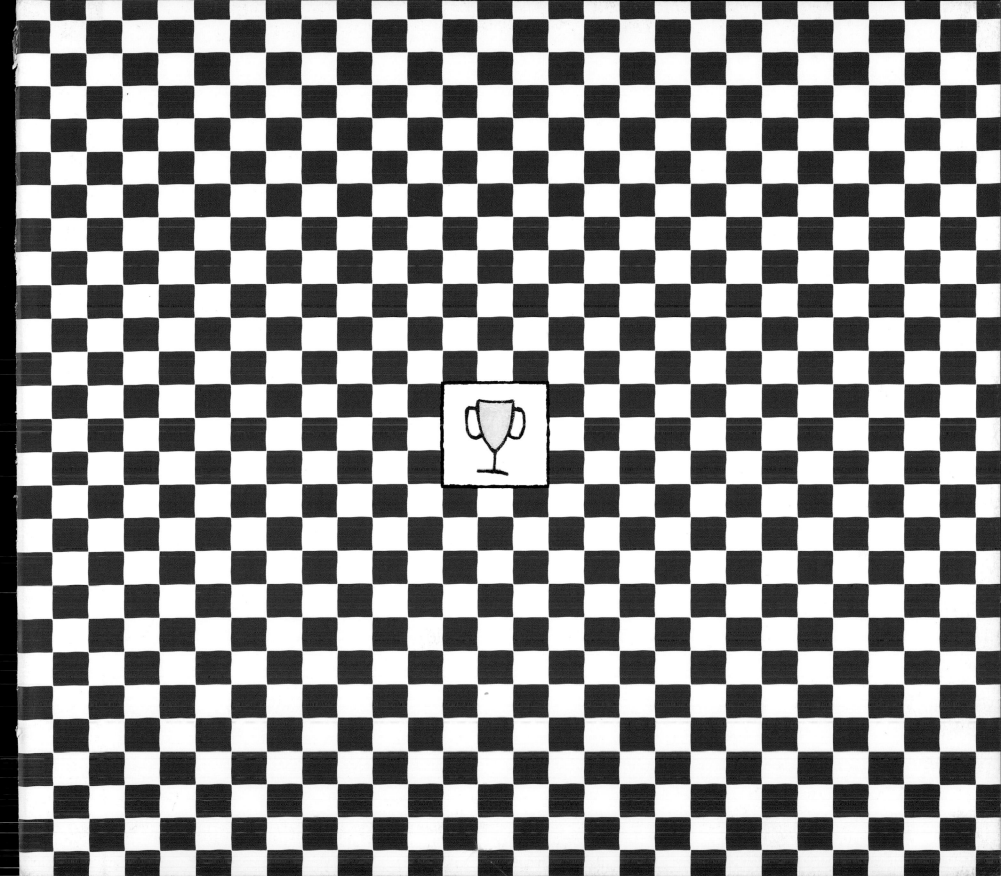

DAYLE ANN DODDS is a former elementary school teacher with a degree in early childhood development. As she does in *The Great Divide,* Dayle Ann Dodds often writes in rhyme because "it is so natural to kids' ears. Rhyme, rhythm, and pattern help kids remember small revelations in entertaining stories," she says. Embedded in the exciting contest of *The Great Divide,* readers will find grouping, adding, subtracting, and multiplying, and discover how they form the foundation of division. Dayle Ann Dodds lives in Carmel Valley, California.

TRACY MITCHELL was born in Boston but grew up in New Orleans, a city whose influence is evident in her art style. *The Great Divide* is her first picture book, and she says that working with such a large number of characters was just one of the many challenges she faced in creating her paintings for the book. "Dividing the racers into crazy groups, like clowns, pirates, and dancers, definitely helped," she says. Tracy Mitchell lives in San Francisco.